D1238001

THREE LECTURES

ON

THE VALUE OF MONEY

AMS PRESS
NEW YORK

THREE LECTURES

ON

THE VALUE OF MONEY,

DELIVERED BEFORE

THE UNIVERSITY OF OXFORD,

IN 1829.

BY NASSAU W. SENIOR, A. M.

PROFESSOR OF POLITICAL ECONOMY,

AND LATE FELLOW OF MAGDALEN COLLEGE.

LONDON:

B. FELLOWES, LUDGATE STREET.

1840.

Library of Congress Cataloging in Publication Data

Senior, Nassau William, 1790-1864.
    Three lectures on the value of money.

    At head of title: Unpublished.
    Reprint of the 1840 ed. published by B. Fellowes,
London.
    1. Money—Addresses, essays, lectures. 2. Precious
metals—Addresses, essays, lectures. I. Title.
HG221.S48   1978   332.4   75-41245
ISBN 0-404-14779-8

Reprinted from an original in the collections
of the University of Connecticut Library

From the edition of 1840, London
First AMS edition published in 1978
Manufactured in the United States of America

AMS PRESS INC.
NEW YORK, N.Y.

ADVERTISEMENT.

SOME of my friends have recommended the publication of the following Lectures; I feel, however, that, after the long period that has passed since they were delivered, they cannot be fit for general circulation until they have been carefully revised—a work for which I have not time at present. As a middle course, I have allowed a few copies to be printed for private distribution. They immediately precede the "Lectures on the Cost of Obtaining Money," which are published.

MASTER'S OFFICES,
Feb. 3, 1840.

LECTURE I.

ON THE QUANTITY AND VALUE OF MONEY.

———————

THE general doctrine is, that the value of money depends partly on its quantity, and partly on the rapidity of its circulation.

"It is not difficult to perceive," says Mr. Mill, "that it is the total amount of the money in any "country which determines what portion of that "quantity shall exchange for a certain portion of "the goods or commodities of that country.

"If we suppose that all the goods of the coun- "try are on one side, all the money on the other, "and that they are exchanged at once against one "another, it is obvious that one-tenth, or one- "hundredth, or any other part of the goods, will "exchange against one tenth, or any other part

" of the whole of the money; and that this tenth,
" &c. will be a great quantity or small, exactly in
" proportion as the whole quantity of the money
" in the country is great or small. If this were
" the state of the facts, therefore, it is evident
" that the value of money would depend wholly
" upon the quantity of it.

" *It will appear that the case is precisely the*
" *same in the actual state of the facts.* The
" whole of the goods of a country are not ex-
" changed at once against the whole of the
" money; the goods are exchanged in portions,
" often in very small portions, and at different
" times during the course of the whole year.
" The same piece of money which is paid in one
" exchange to-day, may be paid in another
" exchange to-morrow. Some of the pieces will
" be employed in a great many exchanges, some
" in a very few, and some, which happen to be
" hoarded, in none at all. There will in all these
" varieties be a certain average number of ex-
" changes, the same which if all the pieces had
" performed an equal number would have been
" performed by each: that average we may

" suppose to be any number we please; say, for
" example, ten. If each of the pieces of money
" in the country perform ten purchases, that is
" exactly the same thing as if all the pieces were
" multiplied by ten, and performed only one pur-
" chase each. As each piece of the money is
" equal in value to that which it exchanges for,
" if each performs ten different exchanges to effect
" one exchange of all the goods, the value of all
" the goods in the country is equal to ten times
" the value of all the money.

" This, it is evident, is a proposition universally
" true. Whenever the value of money has either
" risen or fallen (the quantity of goods against
" which it is exchanged, and the rapidity of
" circulation, remaining the same,) the change
" must be owing to a corresponding diminution
" or increase of the quantity, and can be owing
" to nothing else. If the quantity of goods
" diminish while the quantity of money remains
" the same, it is the same thing as if the quantity
" of money had been increased; and if the quan-
" tity of goods be increased while the quantity of
" money remains unaltered, it is the same thing

" as if the quantity of money had been dimi-
" nished.

" Similar changes are produced by any altera-
" tion in the rapidity of circulation. By rapidity
" of circulation is meant, of course, the number of
" times the money must change hands to effect
" one sale of all the commodities." *

Mr. Mill does not say in so many words that
the value of money is decided by causes differing
from those which decide the value of other commodities; but such is, in fact, the result of the
statement which I have just read, if it be compared with his section on Exchangeable Value.
In that section he states, that " the relative values
" of commodities, in other words, the quantity
" of one which exchanges for a given quantity of
" another, depends entirely upon cost of produc-
" tion." He does not mention rapidity of circulation; or, in other words, a frequent change of
masters; or alteration of actual quantity, except
for short periods, as among the actual elements
of value. And if they are not the principles
which regulate the value of other things, what

* Mill's " Elements of Political Economy," 3d edit. sec. 7.

reason is there for supposing that they regulate the value of money ?

Unless it be maintained that the attributes of gold and silver are changed the instant the metals are divided into portions of a given weight and fineness, and authenticated by a stamp, it must be admitted that their value is governed by the same rules as those which govern the value of all other commodities, produced under similar circumstances. Now the circumstances under which all metals are produced are those of competition, but competition in which the competitors have unequal advantages. They are obtained from alluvial deposits, and mines, all of unequal productiveness. The value of every portion that is produced must, therefore, be sufficient to pay the wages and profits of those who use the least fertile mine, or sift the most poorly impregnated sand, that can be worked without loss. If the value were to rise higher, mines and streams still less productive would be resorted to. If it were to fall lower, the worst now in use would be abandoned. When these principles are applied to native commodities we at once recognise their justice. If

I were to ask why one bushel of wheat will in general exchange for two bushels of barley, any one who had thought on the subject would at once reply, " Because, speaking generally, it costs about as much (or, in my nomenclature, requires the same sum of labour and abstinence) to produce two bushels of barley as one of wheat." But we are not accustomed to consider money as a thing annually produced, and depending for its value on the cost of its production. We talk of it as if nature, or some other equally unknown cause, had diffused a certain amount of it through the country ; and, consistently with such an opinion, ascribe its value solely to its quantity. It appears to me that the only mode of acquiring clear ideas on the subject is to inquire how the value of the precious metals would be fixed under the simplest state of circumstances : and we shall afterwards find that the same causes do, in fact, fix their value under the complicated relations of European society.

It will be necessary, however, to preface this inquiry by some remarks on the causes which determine the quantity of money which a community shall possess.

It is obvious, in the first place, that the whole quantity of money in a community must consist of the aggregate of all the different sums possessed by the different individuals of whom it is constituted.

And what this quantity shall be must depend partly on the number of those individuals; partly on the value in money of the aggregate of their respective incomes; and partly on the average proportion of the value of his income which each individual habitually keeps by him in money.

The two first of these causes do not require much explanation. It is clear, *cœteris paribus*, that two millions of people must possess more money than one million. It is also clear that, *cœteris paribus*, a nation, the value of whose average aggregate income amounts to 100,000,000*l.* sterling a year, must possess more money than one whose annual income is only 50,000,000*l.*

But the causes which determine what proportion of the value of his income each individual shall habitually retain in money require to be considered at some length.

Briefly, it may be said to depend, first, on the proportion to his income of his purchases and sales for money; and secondly, on the rapidity with which they succeed one another: but such a statement is too concise to be intelligible without further explanation.

Exchange, as it is the principal cause, is also one of the principal effects of improvement. As men proceed from a primitive to a refined state of society, as they advance from hunters to shepherds, from shepherds to agriculturists, from villagers to townspeople, and from being inhabitants of towns, depending for their supplies on the adjacent country, to be the citizens of a commercial metropolis, using the whole world as one extensive market;—at each of these stages man becomes more and more a dependent being, consuming less and less of what he individually produces, until at last almost every want, and every gratification, is supplied by means of an exchange. Our ancestors lived on their own estates, fed their households from the produce of their own lands, and clothed them with their own flax and wool, manufactured within their own halls. Food and clothing were the wages of their domestic servants; and their tenants, instead of paying rents in money, were bound to cultivate the lord's demesne, to supply him certain quantities of corn or live-stock, and to serve under his banner in public or private war. The services of the church were obtained by allowing the priest a tenth of the annual produce, and the demands of the state were limited to the maintaining roads and bridges, defence of castles, and attendance in war, for forty days, with adequate provisions. Under such circumstances, the barons and their dependents — and these two classes comprised the bulk of the community—might pass years without having to make a sale or a purchase. Exchanges they made, where one party gave services or produce, and the other party food, clothing, shelter, or land; but these were all made by barter. The yeoman, who cultivated his own land, and used the manufactures of his own family, might, in fact, live without even an exchange ; nor could the serf, though he received maintenance in return for labour, be said to make an exchange, since he had no more power to enforce, or even to require, any stipulation, than any other domestic animal.

The same circumstances must, however, have occasioned what money there was in the country to circulate very slowly; or, in other words, to change hands very unfrequently. A man, who, in such a state of society, received a sum, might not find for a long time an advantageous opportunity of spending it. And he would have many reasons for not parting with it, even on what might appear advantageous terms. Where property and person are so insecure, as they were among our ancestors, every one must feel anxious to have some means of support, if he should be forced to quit his home, or to witness the destruction of his less portable property. Again, the demands for money, when they did come, were great, and unforeseen. The knight was in constant danger of having to pay a ransom; the tenant of having to assist in raising that ransom; and the crown, from time to time, required a subsidy or an escuage.

Under such circumstances it is probable that each individual, or, to speak more correctly, each person managing his own concerns, might on an average receive in money one-fiftieth part of

the value of his annual income. But it is like-
wise probable that what he did so receive he
might retain at an average for four years. Such
a sum would not exceed a month's income; a
very moderate hoard, where the motives for
hoarding were so powerful. I am inclined to
think that the average proportion of their incomes,
which our ancestors hoarded during the first two
or three centuries after the Conquest, was much
larger. It is impossible otherwise to account for
the importance attached to treasure trove, which
seems to have formed a material portion of the
royal revenue, and now probably does not afford,
except from ancient deposits, ten pounds a year.
The whole money of the country would, under
such circumstances, change hands only once in
four years. If we now add to these suppositions
that of a given number of families (meaning by
that word, either single persons managing their
own affairs, or small knots of persons managing
their affairs together, as a man and his wife and
their infant children,) and suppose the average
income of each, we shall have data from which
the whole amount of money in the country may

be inferred. I will suppose, therefore, 500,000 families, having at an average an annual income a-piece of 10*l.* sterling : making the value of the whole annual income of the community 5,000,000*l.* sterling. Each independent person or head of a family is supposed to receive one-fiftieth part of his annual income in money, being 4*s.*, and to keep it in his possession for four years; 16*s.* therefore would be the average sum possessed by each family ; and as there are 500,000 families, sixteen times 500,000, or 8,000,000 of shillings, or 400,000*l.* sterling, would be the whole quantity of money possessed by the community.

It is probable that in this supposition, which is not without resemblance to the state of England under the Norman and Plantagenet lines, I have stated the extremes both of absence of exchange and of slow circulation of money that could take place in a community entitled to be called civilized. We will now suppose the country to be at peace, and secure within and without, and all the peculiar motives for hoarding to be removed. Instead of a month's income, each family might retain only a week's, or 4*s.* instead of 16*s.* Instead of once in four years, the whole money of the country would change hands every year; and 100,000*l.* would perform all the offices of money as well as 400,000*l.* did before. I shall, at a future period, endeavour to show the means by which the stock of money would be diminished to meet the altered state of things; but that it would be diminished must, I think, be at once acknowledged.

Having examined into the causes which determine the quantity of money in any community, I now proceed to inquire into those which determine its value; assuming, what I suppose will not be questioned, that the value of the precious metals, as money, must depend ultimately on their value as materials of jewellery and plate; since, if they were not used as commodities, they could not circulate as money.

I will suppose an insulated society of 10,000 families, having an abundance of land of such fertility, and using manufactures so rude, that the trifling capital employed by them may be disregarded; and so equal in fortune and rank, that the relations of landlord and tenant, and capitalist and workman, shall not exist. I will suppose gold alone to be their money, and that it is obtained by washing alluvial deposits without any expensive machinery or skill, and always in the same ratio to the labour employed.

The cost of producing gold would, under these circumstances, always remain the same, and its value in labour, or, in other words, the amount of labour which a certain quantity of it could purchase, would always correspond with its cost of production, except for short intervals, when any sudden increase or diminution in the demand for it should occasion the existing supply to be for a time relatively excessive or deficient. Under such circumstances the value of all other things would be estimated by comparing their cost of production with that of gold. If the labour of a family employed for a year could gather from the washing places fifty ounces of gold, and by equal exertion gather from the spontaneous produce of the fields fifty quarters of rice, the rice and the gold would be of equal value, and a single quarter of rice would be worth an ounce of gold. If the same labour could produce in the same time one hundred ounces of gold instead of fifty, a quarter of rice would be worth two ounces instead of one ; or if the same labour could gather one hundred quarters of rice instead of fifty, a quarter of rice would be worth only half an ounce instead of a whole ounce ; but while a year's labour could produce just fifty ounces of gold, the yearly income of each family, however employed, supposing their diligence, strength, and skill equal, would be of the value of precisely fifty ounces of gold.

The quantity of gold produced would depend partly on the quantity wanted for plate, including under that word all use of gold except as money, and partly on the quantity wanted for money. The quantity wanted for plate would of course depend on the prevailing fashions of the country : the quantity wanted for money would depend, as we have seen, partly on the value in money of the incomes of all the inhabitants, and partly on the average proportion of the value of his income which each person habitually kept in his possession in money.

If each family cultivated its own land, and prepared its own manufactures, and thus provided for its wants almost without the intervention of exchange, each family would receive in money a very small proportion of the value of its income, and a very small amount of money would be sufficient.

On the other hand, if we suppose each family to be as dependent as an English citizen's on exchange; to part with all its own produce, and to live altogether on what it obtained in return, and at the same time to effect almost all these exchanges, either by means of barter or of accounts regularly kept, and from time to time settled by being balanced against one another, a very small amount of money would again be sufficient.

A much larger quantity would of course be necessary, if we suppose the same prevalence of exchange, but at the same time, the absence of barter and of the balancing of accounts; and consequently suppose the actual use of money in every exchange, and each person to receive in money the whole of his income.

The quantity wanted in that case would depend partly on the cost of producing gold, and partly on the rapidity of its circulation. The rapidity of circulation being given, it would depend on the cost of production. It is obvious that twice as much money would be required to effect every exchange, if a day's labour could obtain from the washing places 34 grains of gold, as would be necessary if a day's labour could obtain only 17. And the cost of production being given, the quantity of money wanted would depend on the rapidity of its circulation.

I have supposed 10,000 families of equal incomes. I will now suppose the cost of producing gold to be such, that a family could gather 118 grains, or what we call a guinea, per week, or about 17 grains per day. Now if the habits of the country were such, that each family lived from hand to mouth, and purchased every day the day's consumption (an impossible supposition, but one which may be used in framing what may be called an intellectual diagram), it is obvious that no family would at an average possess more or less than 17 grains of gold.

170,000 grains, therefore, would be the precise quantity wanted for the purposes of money. And all the money would change hands every day. Let us now consider what would be the consequence if their custom were to make their purchases half-yearly instead of daily. At first sight, we might think that the rapidity of circulation would be retarded in the proportion of 1 to $182\frac{1}{2}$; and, consequently, that rather more than 182 times as much money would be necessary. Such would be the case if each family were on one and the same day to make all their purchases for the ensuing half a year's consumption. But if we suppose them to lay in their stocks of different articles at different times, and at an average to make their purchases and sales, and of course to receive their incomes, on 36 different days during each year, the quantity of money wanted, instead of being 182 times, would not be much more than ten times the former quantity. Each family would, at an average, instead of 17, possess rather more than 170 grains of gold, the whole quantity wanted would rather exceed 1,700,000 grains of gold, and would change hands nearly ten times in a year.

But though any alteration in the rapidity of circulation would much affect the quantity wanted, it would not, except during short periods, affect the value of money while the cost of production remained unaltered. Whether 170,000, or 1,700,000 grains were wanted, still while a day's labour could produce neither more nor less than 17 grains of gold, 17 grains of gold would, except during comparatively short intervals, be the price of every commodity produced by the labour of a day.

I say, except during comparatively short intervals, because though the causes which limit the supply of gold are supposed to be unalterable, those which give it utility, or, in other words, which create the demand for it, might be increased or diminished; and during the interval between the diminution or increase of the demand, and the increase or diminution of the supply in the market, the value might rise above, or sink below, the cost of production.

The primary cause of the utility of gold is, as I have already observed, its use as the material of plate. The secondary cause is its use as money. And in the absence of any disturbing cause, the labour employed in producing gold would be just enough to supply the annual loss and wear of the existing stock of plate and money. Suppose now a change of fashion to occasion a sudden demand for an increased quantity of plate : the introduction, for instance, of the Roman Catholic forms of worship, and a belief in the meritoriousness of adorning every altar with golden candlesticks. That demand would be supplied, partly by melting and converting into candlesticks some of the existing plate, and some of the existing money, and partly by employing on plate all the current supply of gold, a part of which would otherwise have been used as money. The whole quantity of money being diminished, the average quantity possessed by each family must be diminished. A less portion would be offered on every purchase, all prices (except that of plate) would fall, and the monied incomes of all persons, except the gatherers of gold, would be diminished. This of course would occasion much more labour to be employed in gathering gold until the former amount of money were replaced.

If, after this had taken place, the use of plate
should suddenly diminish; if, for instance, pro-
testant forms of worship should supplant the
catholic, the consequences would of course be
precisely opposite. The candlesticks would be
melted down, and the sudden supply of gold
would sink its value. Part of that additional
supply would probably be used as plate, of which
each family could afford to use a little more; the
rest would be turned into money. The whole
quantity of money being increased, each family
would have rather more; rather more would be
offered on every exchange; all prices (except the
price of plate) would rise, and the money incomes
of all persons, except the gatherers of gold, would
be increased. The gathering of gold would, of
course, cease until the gradual loss and wear of
plate and money, uncompensated by any annual
supply, should reduce the quantity of gold below
the amount necessary to supply the existing
demand for plate and money. On the occurrence
of that event, it would again become profitable to
gather gold, and the price of every thing would
again depend on the proportion of the labour

necessary to its production, compared with the labour necessary to obtain a given quantity of gold.

Similar and equally temporary consequences would follow from any causes which should increase or diminish the demand for gold by diminishing or increasing either the use of money in exchange or the rapidity of its circulation.

I will suppose the daily amount of gold that a family can obtain from the washing places to be ten grains, and, consequently, the daily money income of each of the ten thousand families to be 10 grains. Now if such were the habits of the country, as that each family should habitually keep in their possession, at an average, 20 days' income, or 200 grains, the total amount of money in the country would be 2,000,000 grains, and it would change hands about eighteen times every year. If a banker should establish himself, and offer to take charge of that portion of each man's income which was not necessary for immediate use, it is possible that half the money of the country might be deposited with him. Each family might think it safer in his custody than in their own, and would feel the convenience of being able to make payments by drawing on him, and avoiding the trouble of carrying about sums of money. Many exchanges in which money was previously used would now be effected by a mere transfer of credit. A seller would often receive from a purchaser a check, and pay it to the banker, and instead of receiving money for it, merely occasion a certain sum to be taken from the account of the purchaser and placed to that of the seller. If, however, the banker were to keep in his chests all the money deposited with him, one-half of the money would become absolutely stagnant, and the rate of circulation of the whole money in the country might be said to be retarded by one-half; this would precisely balance the effect of the diminution of exchanges for money, and the same quantity of money would be required as before.

We will adopt, however, the more probable supposition, that the banker would keep in his coffers only enough to answer the utmost probable demands of his customers, and employ the remainder either in making purchases himself, or in loans to persons desirous of obtaining commodities or labour, but without sufficient funds of their own. If we suppose him to have received in deposits 1,000,000 grains, or half the money of the country, to retain in his coffers 500,000, and to issue again, in purchases or loans, the remaining 500,000, the effect would be the same as if the existing money of the country were increased by one-fourth. In the first place, there would remain in circulation the 1,000,000 grains undeposited; secondly, there would be the bankers' checks acting as money, and supplying, as instruments of exchange, the million grains deposited; and lastly, there would be 500,000 grains of deposits reissued. The consequence would be, a rise in the price of every commodity except plate, and in the wages of all labourers, except the gatherers of gold. The use of plate would probably be somewhat increased, and the gathering of gold would cease, until the loss and wear of money and plate had reduced the stock of plate to its former amount, and the stock of money to three-fourths of its former amount. If the banker should find the public ready to take his written promise to pay as of equal value with actual payment, and should venture to issue, in purchases and loans, the whole of the 500,000 grains, which we have supposed him to reserve to answer the demands of his customers, this would have the effect of adding one-fourth more to the currency of the country. Prices would again rise, and would not gradually subside to their former level until the unsupplied loss and wear of the gold should have reduced the quantity of money to one half of what had been its amount when the banker began his operations.

If, by this time, it should be discovered that the banker had no reserve to meet the demands of his customers, and the drafts upon him, which before had passed as cash, should become valueless, the same effects would be produced as would have been produced before his establishment, if half the money of the country had been destroyed—had been put, for instance, on board a vessel, and lost at sea. All prices, except the price of plate, and all incomes, except the incomes of the gold gatherers, would fall one half. Plate would be melted into money, and additional labour employed in gathering gold, till the former stock of plate and money were replaced.

My principal object in this long discussion has been to show that the value of money, so far as it is decided by intrinsic causes, does not depend *permanently* on the quantity of it possessed by a given community, or on the rapidity of its circulation, or on the prevalence of exchanges, or on the use of barter or credit, or, in short, on any cause whatever, excepting *the cost of its production.* Other causes may operate for a time, but their influence wears away as the existing stock of the precious metals within the country accommodates itself to the wants of the inhabitants. As long as precisely 17 grains of gold can be obtained by a day's labour, every thing else produced by equal labour will, in the absence of any natural or artificial monopoly, sell for 17 grains of gold; whether all the money of the country change hands every day, or once in four days, or once in four years; whether each individual consume principally what he has himself produced, or supply all his wants by exchange; whether such exchanges are effected by barter or credit, or by the actual intervention of money; whether there be 1,700,000 or 170,000 grains in the country.

In these respects, my insulated community of
10,000 families is a miniature of the whole world.
The whole world may be considered as one community, using gold and silver as money, and
ascertaining the value of other commodities by
comparing their cost of production with the cost
of obtaining gold and silver. And though many
causes may alter the quantity of the precious
metals possessed by any single nation, nothing
will permanently alter their value, so far as that
value depends on intrinsic causes, unless it affect
their cost of production.

In my next Lecture I shall endeavour to show
how the cost of producing the precious metals
may be affected by any increase or diminution of
the demand for them.

LECTURE II.

VALUE OF THE PRECIOUS METALS CONTINUED.

———————

In the last Lecture I inquired how the value of the precious metals would be fixed in the simplest state of circumstances. I supposed the existence of a people without foreign commerce, or valuable capital, using gold as their only money, and obtaining it always in the same proportion to the labour employed. Under such circumstances it appeared that, in the absence of accidental disturbance, or of any natural or artificial monopoly, the relative values of gold, and of any other commodity, would depend solely on the amount of labour necessary to obtain given quantities of each.

I now proceed to inquire how the value of the

precious metals is determined, when the cost of obtaining them is subject to variation. This is a more interesting inquiry, as it is founded, not on hypothesis, but on facts. There are silver mines of every degree of fertility, from those which afford silver as abundantly as the isle of Anglesey does copper, to those in which it would require almost as much exertion as to obtain an equal weight of diamonds. There are sands where a man by a year's labour in washing and sifting can at an average procure 7,000 grains of gold; there are others, still worth working, from which he cannot procure 700, and of course there must be some where he would not get 7. It is an obvious remark that the value of gold and silver, like that of all other produce subjected to a qualified monopoly, must depend, so far as its causes are intrinsic, on the cost of producing it under the least favourable circumstances; or, in other words, on the cost of obtaining that portion which is continued to be obtained at the greatest expense.

But what are the causes which determine what shall be the greatest expense that can be profitably encountered ; or, in other words, what shall be the poorest mine that can be profitably worked ?

The immediate causes are clear. The question whether a given mine shall be worked or abandoned must always be solved by comparing the amount of silver which it produces with the amount of silver which must be expended in working it. If it do not produce more silver than will pay the wages of those who are directly and indirectly employed in working it, it cannot be worked profitably ; if it produce less, it cannot be worked at all ; if the difference be just equal to the current rate of profit in the country, it will just afford to be worked ; if the difference amount to more, it will afford a rent. But this removes the difficulty only a little further, and the reasoning seems to move in a circle. What regulates the wages of labour? The cost of producing silver. On what does the cost of producing silver depend ? On the amount of wages paid to the labourer. Which of these is the cause? which the effect ?

The precious metals are subject to two circumstances by which this puzzle is occasioned. In the first place, the outlay and the return are the same in kind. In this respect, the working of a mine resembles the cultivation of a farm in a society to whom money and barter were unknown. In such a state of society the farmer's expenses would be the same in kind as his returns. He would employ a portion of the annual produce in clothing and maintaining his labourers, feeding his cattle, and sowing and planting his fields, and consider the remainder as his profit; just as the worker of a silver mine employs a portion of the silver produced in making his payments, and keeps the remainder as his profit. But the second peculiarity belongs to the precious metals as money. Nature has fixed a limit below which the farmer's expenditure cannot be reduced. Not less than a certain amount of subsistence is necessary to the existence of his labourers and cattle : if his farm does not produce that amount, it must be abandoned; and even if it do produce that amount, but do not produce a fair profit on the capital expended, it is a losing concern. The utility of bread is not in proportion to its cost of production. Because a loaf of bread cost ten times as much labour as it does now, it would not feed ten times as many people. If we could obtain one, at one-tenth of its present cost, we should not want to eat ten times as many. But the utility of any given amount of money is in exact proportion to its cost of production. If that were to fall to one-twentieth, just twenty times as much money as before would be required for every purchase. If it were twenty times as difficult to procure a given quantity, that quantity would perform all the functions of money just as well as twenty times the quantity did before. In the first case, sovereigns would be used as shillings, in the second case shillings as sovereigns. It appears, therefore, that it is the cost of producing money which determines the demand for it, rather than the demand for it which decides to what extent the production shall be carried.

But if it be not the demand for the precious metals as money which decides what shall be the least productive mine that can be profitably worked, what *is* the cause which so decides?

Ultimately and principally the demand for them as commodities; as the materials of plate, gilding and jewellery; and through the intervention, and as a consequence of that demand, the demand for them as money.

I am sorry to say that I cannot make this clear without supposing given amounts of money and plate, requiring given annual supplies, and mines of different fertilities : in fact, without entering into hypothetical calculations which it may be difficult to follow. My apology is, first, that those among my hearers who can manage to follow them will, I think, find that they make the subject clear; and, secondly, that I do not believe that there are any other means of satisfactorily explaining it.

I will suppose a country without foreign commerce, using no precious metal excepting silver, and obtaining it from mines of different degrees of fertility. Without inquiring into the causes by which such a state of things has been occasioned, I will suppose that country to contain 24,000 ounces of plate, and 12,000 ounces of money ; and that to keep up the plate requires an annual supply of 2,000 ounces, and to keep up the money, an annual supply of 800 ounces. I will suppose the average rate of profit to be one-tenth or about eleven per cent. per annum, and that the wages of all persons, directly or indirectly employed in producing silver, whom I will call by the general name of miners, must at an average be advanced for a year before the silver produced by them can be made use of.

I will suppose there to be five mines, one from which 50 miners can annually obtain 1100 ounces; a second, from which 50 miners can annually obtain 900 ounces; a third, from which the same number of miners can obtain 800 ounces; a fourth, producing with the same labour 600 ounces, and a fifth, giving only 400 ounces.

Now as the annual supply necessary to keep up the stock of plate and money is 2,800 ounces, it is clear that the three best mines only, which together produce precisely the quantity wanted, can be worked. It is also clear that the value of silver must depend on the cost of producing it at the third, or least fertile mine. At that mine, 50 miners can annually produce 800 ounces. As their wages are advanced for a year, and the profit taken by the capitalist is one-tenth, 80 of these 800 ounces go to the capitalist, and the remaining 720 are retained by the miners. Each of the 50 miners annually raises 16 ounces of silver, out of which he receives $14\frac{2}{5}$ for his wages, and gives up $1\frac{3}{5}$ to the capitalist. At the second mine, each miner annually raises 18 ounces. But as neither the labourer nor the capitalist have any claim to greater wages, or to a greater profit at one mine than at another, the miner still receives $14\frac{2}{5}$ ounces, the capitalist $1\frac{3}{5}$ ounces, and the remaining 2 ounces must be taken by the proprietor of the mine as his rent. At the first, or most fertile mine, each miner raises 22 ounces, of which he retains, as before, $14\frac{2}{5}$, gives $1\frac{3}{5}$ to the capitalist, and the remaining 6 to the proprietor. The best mine yields a rent of 300 ounces, the second a rent of 100 ounces, the third can just be profitably worked, and the fourth and fifth are useless. Under these circumstances $14\frac{2}{5}$ ounces of silver must be the average annual wages of labour, and 16 ounces the price of every commodity produced under circumstances of equal competition by a year's labour; the labourer's wages having been advanced for a year: and the pivots on which all the money transactions of the country turn, are the existence of persons able and willing to give for 16 ounces of plate, the commodities produced by the labour of one man for a year, his wages having been advanced for a year, and the power of the miner to raise, without payment of rent, 16 ounces of silver by a year's labour; in short, the amount of silver required, and the cost of producing that portion of it which is produced at the greatest expense.

I am sorry to say that the only mode by which the truth of these propositions can be demonstrated, is by a new series of calculations exhibiting the influence on prices of any increase or diminution in the demand for plate or money.

I will suppose the demand for silver, as a commodity, to diminish, by the substitution of plain for embroidered clothes: a substitution which would not occasion any of the existing plate to be converted into money, but would enable the stock to be kept up by a much smaller annual

supply. I will suppose the change such as that
300 ounces a year instead of 2,000 shall be sufficient to keep up the existing stock.

We supposed at the outset an annual demand
of 800 ounces for money, making, with the 300
ounces now required for plate, 1,100 ounces ; and
we supposed 1,100 ounces to be annually supplied from the best mine by the labour of 50
men. It may be thought that the best mine
would now be the only mine worth working :
and such would be the case, if it were possible
that the quantity of silver required for money
could remain the same after the cost of producing
it had fallen more than one-third. If the best
mine alone were worth working, the proprietor
would receive no rent, and of the 22 ounces
annually raised from it by each miner, the
capitalist would receive one-tenth, or $2\frac{1}{5}$ ounces,
and each miner $19\frac{4}{5}$ ounces. There would be a
general rise of the wages of labour from $14\frac{2}{5}$ ounces
to $19\frac{4}{5}$ ounces, and as the cost of production of
silver alone would be diminished, all prices would
have a tendency to rise in the same proportion.
This, however, they could not do immediately,

as the 12,000 ounces current as money would be incapable of effecting all the exchanges in which they are supposed to be necessary, if the sum payable on each exchange were increased one-third. It would, therefore, still be necessary to work the second mine, from which we have supposed each miner to obtain 18 ounces of silver a year. If no rent were paid, he would give one-tenth of this amount, or $1\frac{4}{5}$ to the capitalist, and retain $16\frac{1}{5}$ ounces for himself. But as one-eighth more money would be necessary to allow of a general rise of prices of one-eighth, the full rise could not take place till the stock of money had been increased by one-eighth, or from 12,000 ounces to 13,500 ounces. In a little more than a year this would be effected, as the annual produce of the two best mines is 2,000 ounces, and the reduced annual consumption only 1,100. In the meantime, although the fall in the value of money, or, in other words, the rise in the wages of labour, must have instantly thrown the third mine out of work; the second would continue to afford a rent, constantly diminishing, as wages gradually rose from $14\frac{2}{3}$ ounces a year, till the 13,500 ounces of money being obtained, they reached $16\frac{1}{5}$ ounces. The second mine would then afford only average wages and profit, and could pay no rent; it still, however, must be worked, as the best mine, producing only 1,100 ounces, would not be sufficient to supply the annual waste of plate, and of the increased quantity of money. But the second mine could not be worked to its former extent; for if more were produced from it than just enough to keep up, with the assistance of the best mine, the annual waste of plate and money, the increase would sink the value of money, the wages of the miner would rise, and the second mine would no longer be worth working. But while the existing demand for plate and money continued the same, and the second mine was worked to a proper extent, its productiveness would regulate the value in silver of labour, and of every other commodity or service. The average annual wages of labour would be $16\frac{1}{5}$ ounces; the average price of every commodity produced by one man's labour for a year, his wages having been advanced for a year, would be 18 ounces; and the best mine, in which a year's labour, so assisted, produces 22 ounces, would afford the difference as a rent to its proprietor.

We will now reverse the supposition, and shew the effects of an increased use of plate. It may be well first to recal to your recollection that I originally supposed a stock of plate, consisting of 24,000 ounces, and 12,000 ounces of money; requiring an annual supply, the first of 2,000 ounces, and the second of 800, and the existence of five mines, capable of supplying, by the labour of 50 men each, the first 1,100 ounces, the second 900 ounces, the third 800 ounces, the fourth 600 ounces, and the fifth 400 ounces. I will now suppose such an increase in the demand for plate as to require an annual supply of 2,800 ounces instead of 2,000 ounces, making, with the 800 required to keep up the stock of money, 3,600 ounces. Now as the four first mines produce altogether only 3,400 ounces, it might appear that it would be necessary to work the fifth mine. From that mine each labourer can raise, by a year's labour, only 8 ounces, of which, at the current rate of profit, he would keep $7\frac{1}{5}$ ounces for his wages, and give to the capitalist the remaining four-fifths of an ounce as profit. But it is clear, in the first place, that until wages had fallen one-half, or from $14\frac{2}{5}$ ounces to $7\frac{1}{5}$ ounces, the fifth mine could not be worked; as the persons employed on it would otherwise receive more silver as wages and profits than they raised as ore; and it is also clear that wages could not fall one-half, while the stock of money remained undiminished. It is also clear that that stock would be diminished. The increased demand for silver, as a commodity, would instantly cause a portion of the money to be converted into plate; all prices, and among them the miners' wages, would fall; he would no longer be able to retain $14\frac{2}{5}$ ounces out of the 16, which he is supposed to raise from the third mine. That mine would immediately afford a rent to its proprietor; but it would not be profitable to work the fourth mine until the wages of labour had fallen one-fourth, or from $14\frac{2}{5}$ ounces to $10\frac{4}{5}$ ounces; at any higher rate the capitalist must give up his profit, or the ore sell for more than the silver it contained. But as the stock of money was gradually reduced by the conversion of a portion of it into plate, and by its annual waste unsupplied from the mines, it would at last sink from 12,000 ounces to 9,000 ounces, requiring the annual supply of 600 instead of 800 ounces. Prices would now be sufficiently reduced to allow the fourth mine to be opened. Its produce, added to that of the three first mines, would amount to 3,400 ounces, and would exactly supply the annual waste of 2,800 ounces of plate, and 600 of money. The cost of producing silver from the fourth mine would now be the regulator of prices ; the average annual wages of labour would be $10\frac{4}{5}$ ounces ; and every commodity produced, under circumstances of equal competition, by the labour of one man for a year, his wages having been advanced for a year, would sell for 12 ounces of silver.

It appears, therefore, that any increase or diminution in the demand for plate occasions an increase or diminution of the demand for silver in the same direction, and a diminution or increase in the demand for money in an inverse direction.

An increased demand for money must, in a similar manner, increase the demand for silver and diminish the demand for plate, and *vice versâ*. To make this clear, I must recur to my hypothesis.

We supposed the existence of 24,000 ounces of plate and 12,000 of money; the plate requiring an annual supply of 2,000 ounces, and the money of 800 ounces. We will suppose that the circulation of the country in question consisted, in addition to the 12,000 of money, of government paper of the nominal value of 18,000 ounces, and equally esteemed: making altogether a currency of 30,000 ounces. We will now suppose a political revolution suddenly and completely to deprive the paper of its value, and, consequently, to reduce the currency of the country from 30,000 to 12,000 ounces. If it were possible that the use of plate and of money could remain unaltered, all the five mines might now be worked; and the fifth mine, at which each miner raises 8 ounces, of which $7\frac{1}{5}$ are his wages, and $\frac{4}{5}$ the capitalist's profit, would regulate the price of every commodity and service. But it is impossible that the use of plate could be unaffected, after the cost of obtaining it had doubled. To what extent its use would be diminished cannot be ascertained: we will suppose it, however, to be diminished one-fourth. In that case one-fourth of the existing plate, or 6,000 ounces, would immediately be converted into money; making, with the previous 12,000 ounces, 18,000 ounces. This would be enough to prevent the value of money from doubling, an event which must precede the working of the fifth mine. As the 18,000 ounces of silver would have to perform the exchanges formerly effected by 30,000 of silver and notes, they would rise in value two-fifths: this would allow the fourth mine not only to be worked, but to afford a rent to its proprietor, since the wages of labour would have fallen two-fifths, and that mine is only one-fourth less productive than the third. And this state of things would continue until there should exist 22,500 ounces of money, equal, after allowing for a rise in value of one-fourth, to the former 30,000 ounces. To keep up this stock of money, would, at the assumed rate of wear, require an annual supply of 1,500 ounces, and precisely the same annual supply would be required to keep up the stock of plate; in all, 3,000 ounces. As the three best mines supply only 2,800 ounces, the fourth must be worked; and its productiveness would regulate the value in silver of all commodities and services.

It is scarcely necessary to show that the re-introduction of notes, or of any substitute for money, would diminish the value of plate and money, and throw the fourth, and perhaps the third, mine out of work; that this very diminution of the value of silver would increase the use of plate, and, by raising prices, would make a greater quantity of money necessary on those occasions in which money was actually used, until, after oscillations continuing for a shorter or a longer period, the joint demand for plate and money should again decide what should be the least productive mine that could be profitably worked.

My next Lecture will be a continuation of the present subject.

LECTURE III.

In my last Lecture, I considered the influence which any increase or diminution in the use of plate or money would have on the cost of producing silver. I will now inquire into the results which would follow from any increase or diminution of the productiveness of the existing mines; and I must again recur to my hypothetical country, and its varying mines. We supposed as you may recollect, five mines. One producing annually 1,100 ounces, at the rate of 22 ounces to a miner; one, 900 ounces, at the rate of 18 ounces to a miner; one, 800 ounces, at the rate of 16 ounces to a miner; one, 600 ounces, at the rate of 12 ounces to a miner; and one, 400 ounces, at the rate of 8 ounces to a miner. We supposed the capitalist's profit

to amount to one-tenth of the produce, and
we supposed the existence of 24,000 ounces of
plate and 12,000 ounces of money; the plate
requiring an annual supply of 2,000 ounces, and
the money of 800 ounces; and, as an inference
from these premises, it appeared that the first
three mines alone would be worked. I will now
suppose that the best mine, producing annually
1,100 ounces, is suddenly and irretrievably filled
with water. The increase of the obstacles to the
supply of plate would immediately increase its
value; that is, would make the community
willing to make greater sacrifices to obtain a
given quantity of it, while the absolute quantity
wanted would be diminished, as fewer persons
would be capable of affording to purchase it, and
those who could would purchase it to a smaller
amount. There are no means of deciding at
what point the demand for plate would ultimately
settle; but the immediate effect of the increase
on the value of silver would be, that a portion of
the 12,000 ounces of money would be melted to
supply, with the 1,700 ounces still annually produced from the second and third mines, the wear

of plate. The silver wages of the miner would fall, the rent of the second mine would rise, the third mine would afford a rent, and the fourth would probably be worth working. As the wear of both plate and money would considerably exceed the whole supply of silver, all prices except the price of plate would continue gradually to fall until the value of plate, compared with other things, had reached the point at which the community refused to make any greater sacrifice to keep up their existing stock. If this point were such as to occasion the fourth mine to be the worst in use, the ultimate results would be exactly similar to those which I have described as following an increase of the consumption of plate from 2,000 ounces to 2,800 ounces, except that there would be less plate.

Suppose the proposition reserved, and, instead of the destruction of a mine, the discovery of one, from which 50 miners can produce annually 3,000 ounces or 60 ounces per miner. In this case, as in the last, it is impossible to say at what point the demand for plate would settle. All that can be safely laid down is, that the community would no longer be willing to make the same sacrifices to obtain a given quantity of plate ; and that the absolute quantity wanted would be increased, as more people would be able to afford to use a given quantity. The value of silver having diminished, the third mine must instantly go out of work ; but, as more silver would become necessary as money, the second mine would still continue to give a rent, which would gradually diminish as the accumulation of plate and money occasioned a gradual fall in the value of plate ; and rise in the silver wages of labour, until the increased annual wear of the increased quantity of plate and money having become equal to the annual supply of silver, the market for silver would again be in a settled state.

It appears from this analysis that the demands for plate and money are antagonist demands, and, in a great measure, neutralize one another : that an increased consumption of plate, by raising the value of silver, occasions less money to be necessary ; and though, by reducing the silver wages of the miner, it enables a worse mine to be worked, yet the supply which may be obtained by melting money, and the diminution of the use of silver as money, keep inactive the mine which must have been employed if the former quantity of money had still been required : that a diminished demand for plate, by sinking the value of silver, makes more money necessary ; and though, by increasing the silver wages of the miner, it throws the worst mine out of use, its effect is checked by the conversion of plate into money, and by the increase of the annual waste of the increased quantity of money ; and that the effects of an increase or diminution in the use of money are equally checked, the one by the increased relative efficiency of the money obtained at a greater cost, and the other by the diminished relative efficiency of the money which has cost less labour : and that, in all cases, the proximate cause which determines whether a given mine shall or shall not be worked is the difference between the average silver wages of labour, and the silver which a given quantity of labour will extract from it ; if that amounts to the average profit of capital for the time for which the wages must be

advanced, the mine is worked; if not, abandoned.

It is a remarkable fact, particularly with refe-
rence to the opinion that the value of money
depends on its quantity, that while the fertility
of the mines is unaltered, every increase of the
total amount of silver is preceded by an increase
of its value, indeed, could not take place, unless
so preceded; and that every diminution of the
value of silver is followed by a diminution of the
whole quantity. A striking illustration of the
principle that, although value depends principally on limitation of supply, it is regulated not
by the actual amount of the supply, but by the
comparative force of the obstacles by which the
supply is limited. And that, if those obstacles
are increased, as must be the case whenever an
increase of demand forces an increased cost of
production to be incurred, the whole quantity
produced, and the value of each portion of that
quantity, will increase together.

It will be observed that, throughout this discussion, I have considered the wages of the
miner as regulating the remuneration of every

other labourer. You are of course aware that
the wages of labour vary, in every occupation
according to the lightness or severity of the toil
and risk to be encountered. The easiest, the
healthiest, and, in every way, the most agreeable
labour in which man can be employed, seems
to be his primeval task of tilling the ground.
On the other hand, the occupation of a miner
is eminently severe, unhealthy, and dangerous.
The consequence is, that the wages of agricul-
tural labour are always the lowest that are paid,
and those of mining among the highest. In
Mexico the wages of the miner are about double
those of the cultivator. But it is clear that the
wages of the miner must afford the scale by
which all other wages are regulated. When
once experience has ascertained the comparative
advantages and disadvantages of different occu-
pations, they will continue to bear, as to wages,
the same proportion to one another. A fall in
the cost of producing silver must raise the money-
wages of the miner. If those of the agriculturist
did not rise in proportion, the miner's wages
would be more than in proportion to his sacri-

fices, and they would be reduced by the consequent competition. And, on the other hand, mining would be abandoned, if, when the cost of producing silver is increased, the wages in other employments could be stationary.

I am happy to say that I have now done with my hypothetical illustration, and can proceed to a practical question ; namely, to inquire what are the causes which actually decide the cost at which silver shall be produced. To simplify the question, it will be best to exclude all mines except those of Mexico, which, in fact, furnish five-sixths of the whole supply, and not to take into consideration the present state of that country, but to treat it as if still in the same state as when left by Humboldt, twenty-five years ago.*

The question, thus simplified, will be to ascertain the causes which, when Humboldt left Mexico, decided what should be the least productive mine that could be profitably worked.

The immediate causes are clear. The question whether a given mine shall be worked or abandoned must always be solved by comparing the

* This Lecture was delivered in 1829.

amount of silver which it produces with the amount of silver which must be expended in working it; or, to speak more in detail, by ascertaining—

First, The average quantity of silver which it periodically supplies.

Secondly, The average quantity of silver expended in paying the wages of the workmen directly employed about it.

Thirdly, The average quantity of silver expended in paying those who indirectly assist in working it; a payment which includes the expenses of government.

Fourthly, The average quantity of silver expended in paying for the mercury, steel, and other foreign commodities necessary for the work.

Fifthly, The average time for which these payments must be made in advance.

Sixthly, The average profit which the capitalist who makes all these advances could obtain by any other employment of his capital.

If the silver obtained is just sufficient to answer all these payments, the mine will be worked; if it be more, the mine will yield a rent; if less, it will be abandoned.

But such an answer gives no real information. There are in Mexico mines of every intermediate degree of fertility, between that of Sombrerete, which in six months gave its proprietor a net profit of 800,000$l.$, and probably afforded silver at a less expense than copper costs in Wales; and those which, if worked, would require as much labour as is necessary to obtain platina or gold.

The first thing to be ascertained is the aggregate quantity of silver annually required.

If the market for Mexican silver were confined to Mexico, we have seen that the demand for plate would ultimately determine the aggregate quantity of silver annually required. But Humboldt (lib. vi. cap. 4,) calculates that only $\frac{1}{23}$d of the silver produced in Mexico is consumed in that country: the whole annual amount he estimates (lib. iv. cap.1,) at 1,640,000 lbs. troy, equal in value to about 5,000,000$l.$ sterling. Of this, about 71,304 lbs., or about 217,000$l.$ sterling, is retained by the Mexicans for their own use; the remaining 1,568,696 lbs., or 4,783,000$l.$ sterling, they export. Taking the Valenciana mine as standard, in which 3,100 labourers earned annually 3,400,000 livres (Humboldt, lib. iv. cap. 11,) we find the silver wages of the Mexican miner to be, or rather to have been when Humboldt wrote, about 44*l.* sterling, or about 178 ounces of silver a-year. If we add about a third more for the wages of the persons indirectly employed in assisting the miners, as producers of tallow, powder, quicksilver, and the other tools of the miner, we must add about 60 ounces more as the silver which each miner must produce, making together 238 ounces. It is difficult to estimate the average time for which the wages of these workmen must be advanced, or the average rate of profit in Mexico, but I will suppose the average period of advance to be two years, and the average rate of profit to be one-seventh per annum. The wages of one miner and one-third more having, therefore, been advanced for two years, we must add 73 ounces more for profit, making altogether 311 ounces.

If these data are correct, and, as they are assumed merely for the purpose of illustration, it does not signify whether they are correct or not, it was necessary, in order to produce annually in

Mexico 1,640,000 lbs. troy of silver, to work mines of different degrees of fertility, down to that at which each miner, his wages, and the wages of those who assist him, having been advanced for two years, produced annually 311 ounces; and all mines more productive yielded a rent; all less productive were losing concerns. If more silver had been required, it could have been obtained; but a worse mine must have been worked, and the silver wages of the miner would have sunk; if less had been required, a better mine would have become the worst mine in activity, and the silver wages of the miner would have risen.

What was it, then, which decided that 1,640,000 lbs. should be the quantity annually required? Not the want of plate in Mexico, for they required annually for their own use only 71,304 lbs., a quantity so small that it may be left out of calculation. The determining causes must have been that such was the desire of the inhabitants of the rest of the world for silver, and such their powers of producing commodities desired by the Mexicans, and such the desire of the Mexicans for the commodities produced by the rest of the world, and such their power of producing silver, that the rest of the world offered annually to Mexico commodities sufficient to induce the Mexicans to produce annually for exportation 1,568,696 lbs. troy of silver, and the Mexicans offered annually to the rest of the world 1,568,696 lbs. troy of silver, in return for the commodities which were annually produced by it for the Mexican market.

And any alteration in one of these determining causes, unless neutralized by a compensating alteration in another, would produce a corresponding alteration in the value of silver. If the taste for plate in the rest of the world, or to use a more concise expression, in Europe and Asia (for Africa and the rest of America influence the question so slightly that they may be omitted) should diminish, and the Mexicans should not be willing to sacrifice more labour and capital for the purpose of keeping up their consumption of foreign commodities ; as fewer commodities would be offered to Mexico in exchange for silver, less silver would be exported ; the accumulation of silver in Mexico would sink its value; the silver wages of the miner would rise; the worst mines would be thrown out of work; and the persons formerly employed in working them would be employed in making substitutes for the foreign commodities now no longer imported, as being no longer to be obtained at the same cost. And though less silver would be produced, yet as the demand for it would be reduced, and as the worst mine in use, which may be called the regulating mine, would be a more productive mine, the value of silver would fall over the whole world, though its fall would be checked by the increased use of it as money, occasioned by its diminished efficiency. And it is a remarkable circumstance, that all wages and prices would be raised in Mexico by the injury of the most important branch of her commerce.

I will now suppose a diminution in the power of Asia and Europe to produce commodities desired by Mexico. Suppose the Mexicans to discover a mode of fabricating at home, at a less expense, half of the commodities which they previously imported; and that Europe and Asia

are not immediately willing to make additional
sacrifices to obtain silver. The Mexicans would,
in this case also, turn a part of their miners into
producers of other commodities, but with this
difference, that, instead of losing, they would
benefit by the change. They would become independent of foreign supply, in the only mode
in which such an independence is beneficial;
not through unwillingness or inability to purchase
abroad, but by being able to produce more easily
at home. As to silver, however, the results to
them would be precisely the same as in the last
example, the regulating mine would be a better
mine, and all prices in silver would rise. But in
Europe and Asia the effect would be very different. As less silver would be imported, and as
the deficiency in the supply had not been preceded by a diminution in the demand, its value
would rise; this would occasion, to a certain
extent, a reaction in Mexico, and some of the
mines which had at first been abandoned would
be resumed; but the ultimate result would be that
prices would be higher in Mexico, and lower in
the rest of the world, than before the first altera-

tion took place. Mexico would produce less and yet retain more silver than before; a service of plate would be cheaper there and dearer in Europe and Asia, and it would require more silver in Mexico and less in Europe and Asia to perform the exchanges previously performed by a given quantity of money.

It is to be observed, that, in both the cases which I have put, the worst mines would be thrown out of use. Yet, in the first example, the value of money falls in Europe and Asia; and, in the second, it rises. The cause of this difference is that, in the first example, while the demand for silver is diminished in Europe and Asia, the force of the obstacle which limits its supply there, that is, the sum of labour and abstinence necessary to obtain a given quantity of it from Mexico, is not varied. In the second case, while the demand for it is not diminished, the force of the obstacle to its supply in Europe and Asia is increased. And that increase ultimately resolves itself into an increased value of Mexican labour.

I will now consider the circumstances which

would occasion a less productive mine to be worked.

If the taste for plate should increase in Europe and Asia, more commodities would be offered to Mexico in exchange for silver. It would become profitable in Mexico to direct a portion of their labour and capital to the production of an increased quantity. As this must be obtained from a worse mine, the silver wages of the miner, and all other prices, would fall in Mexico, as, to obtain the further quantity of silver, they must have previously fallen in Europe and Asia. The prices of *commodities* would probably fall more in Mexico than in Europe and Asia, because the whole amount of commodities in Mexico would be increased, and in Europe and Asia diminished. But the price of *labour* would probably fall more in Europe and Asia than in Mexico; for the demand in Europe and Asia for the produce of Mexican labour having increased, the results of a given quantity of Mexican labour would command in exchange the results of a larger quantity of European and Asiatic labour than before.

If instead of an increased taste in Europe and

Asia for plate, we suppose an increased taste in Mexico for European and Asiatic commodities, the Mexicans would be forced to increase their export of silver. This they could only do by working a less productive mine: prices and wages would fall in Mexico, while the increase in the quantity of silver imported would raise them in Europe and Asia; and the ultimate consequence would be, that the results of a given quantity of European and Asiatic labour would command in exchange the results of more Mexican labour than before.

The consequences in Europe and Asia of an increase or diminution in the fertility of the Mexican mines have been so much anticipated, that they may appear not to require a minute investigation, but they are too important to be slightly passed over.

The whole number of miners in Mexico was estimated by Humboldt at 30,000. It is probable that he included only those directly employed in extracting the ore. I will assume for the purpose of illustration, that there was then an equal number of persons whose whole labour was employed indirectly for the same purpose, making together 60,000. We have seen that they then annually produced 1,640,000 lbs. troy of silver : the produce of the rest of the world is supposed to be one-fifth more, or 328,000 lbs. ; making together an annual supply of 1,968,000 lbs., or in round numbers, 2,000,000 lbs. The whole quantity of silver now in use in the world appears, on an average of the different estimates, to be about 600,000,000 lbs. troy ; and as the quantity does not appear to increase, the production and consumption probably balance one another, and the whole quantity is consumed and reproduced in 300 years. I will suppose Humboldt's calculation to be correct, and that one-third of the whole quantity, or about 200,000,000 lbs. is used as plate, and two-thirds, or about 400,000,000 lbs. as money : but as the waste of silver in plate is more rapid than in money, it is probable that they divide the annual supply between them, and that 1,000,000 lbs. troy is annually required to keep up the existing quantity of plate, and about the same quantity to keep up the stock of money.

I will now suppose a set of mines to be discovered in Mexico, from which 10,000 men, their wages having been advanced for a year, annually produce 2,000,000 lbs. of silver. If it were possible that the desire for silver plate in the whole world, Mexico included, should increase so as to absorb the whole of this additional quantity of silver for the purposes of plate, very little effect would be produced. The value of plate in labour and in other commodities would be unaltered; the annual supply of plate, and the annual expense to the consumers of obtaining the additional supply now annually obtained by them, would each of them be rather more than trebled; and as the expense of procuring silver from the new mines would bear a small proportion to its value, their proprietors would derive a very large rent. It is clear, however, that this sudden increase of demand for plate would not take place, for, as we have supposed the price not to fall, there would be no motive for it.

The immediate effect of the additional supply of silver would certainly be a fall in its value, but a very trifling one, as the additional quantity offered in the first year could be only $\frac{1}{300}$th part of the existing mass of silver in the market. I do not think that the fall in the value of plate, which so slight an addition would occasion, would be sufficient to increase the quantity consumed. The whole additional quantity of silver would therefore be employed as money, and would be an addition of one-half per cent. to the existing quantity. Such an addition would scarcely occasion a perceptible rise of prices for the first, or even the second year. By the sixth year, however, it would amount to three per cent. and unquestionably, all prices and wages, and, among others, the wages of the miners, would have a tendency to rise. The rise would, however, be checked by a slight increase in the consumption of plate, which, probably, after the fourth or fifth year, would attract about the same proportion of the increased supply as it does of the present supply, leaving 1,000,000 lbs. or one-fourth per cent. to be annually added to the stock of money. Even at this rate, however, in twenty years there would be an increase in the stock of money, and a rise of prices and wages of only five per cent.

The worst mines would now cease to be worked. To what extent this would check the depreciation caused by the newly discovered mines would depend on the quantity of silver which had been annually produced by the mines abandoned. If this had amounted to 200,000 lbs. the operation of the newly discovered mines would be weakened by one-tenth. It would require twenty-two years more before there could be a further addition of five per cent. to the existing stock of money, and a further abandonment of the mines now become the worst in use. In the mean time, the increase in the annual wear of the increased quantity of plate and money would begin to show itself, and would again diminish the effect of the new mines; and the operation of the new mines, in adding to the existing stock of money, would thus be gradually diminished, until a point was reached, at which the annual supply and consumption of silver would be equal. The value of silver would then be stationary, and the only result of the discovery would be, that plate would be more easily obtained, and all prices and wages estimated in silver would be higher than before.

Such must have been the steps by which, when first the American mines were worked, the greater part of the European mines became unprofitable, and by which the mines of Potosi afterwards occasioned the earlier American mines to be abandoned.

The effects of a diminished fertility of the mines would be equally gradual. Suppose, when the Mexican mines were annually producing 1,640,000 lbs. of silver, a popular insurrection had suddenly and irretrievably destroyed the works of mines producing annually 1,000,000 lbs. As the existing stock of plate and money would in the subsequent year suffer its usual waste of 2,000,000 lbs. and receive a supply of only 1,000,000 lbs. the existing stock would be diminished by $\frac{1}{600}$th part. So slight a diminution would not perceptibly diminish the consumption of plate. The whole annual supply would therefore be converted into plate, and the waste of money, which we have computed at 1,000,000 lbs. or $\frac{1}{200}$th part, would not be replaced. As soon as the reduction in the quantity of money was sufficient to raise its value, and sink the wages of the miner, a mine less productive than the worst previously in use might be worked. But, by this time, the increased cost of plate would somewhat check its consumption ; instead of attracting all the supply of silver, it would again divide it with money. Still, while the waste continued greater than the supply, worse and worse mines would be gradually brought into use, until the gradual increase of the supply, and diminution of the waste, should bring them back to balance one another. The value of silver would then again be stationary, and the only ultimate result would be, that prices in silver would be rather lower, and that plate would cost more than before.

The slowness with which any alteration in the productiveness of the mines shews itself is strikingly proved by the fact, that civil disturbances have rendered the Mexican mines almost totally unproductive for the last fifteen years, so much so indeed, that silver has been sent to Mexico from Europe, and yet neither the general value of silver, nor its specific value in gold, has suffered any perceptible alteration.

I must add that, to simplify the question, I have

omitted a circumstance which must considerably retard the operation of any increase or diminution in the demand for silver in increasing or diminishing its supply; and that is, the quantity of fixed capital, which in every mine forms a considerable portion of the expense, and in the poorest, or, in other words, the most expensive mines, is the principal expense. The piercing and walling of three draught-pits in the Valenciana mine cost 240,000*l.*; and in 1803, the date of Humboldt's account of that mine (lib. iv. c. 11), another draught-pit had been for twelve years in progress, which was expected to cost 212,000*l.*, and to be completed about the year 1815. The haciendos de beneficio, or works for reducing the ores, are also buildings of great extent and expense; those belonging to the Real del Monte mine are stated, in an account of that mine appended to the third report of the Real del Monte company, to have cost 527,000 dollars. In the same report, the adit to these mines, or passage for draining them, is said to have been thirteen years in progress, and to have cost 1,000,000 dollars; and we know that the different companies succeeding to mines, in which an enormous amount of fixed capital has been already invested, have spent very large sums, and as yet obtained scarcely any returns. Such capitals resemble bodies which require a long continued impulse to set them in motion, and continue to move long after that impulse has been withdrawn.

Though the cessation for fifteen years of all supply from America must have increased the demand for silver; and though the different mining companies have possessed for some years the principal mines,—mines which, under a heavy taxation, and worked with inferior skill, yielded immense rents, besides profits much beyond the European standard; yet, with all these stimulants, scarcely any silver has yet reached us from Mexico.* On the other hand, when the Real del Monte company have expended 2,000,000*l.* and six years in completing works which have already cost millions to the Regla family, they certainly will continue to work them, although, as is very probable, the

* This was said in 1829.

silver they extract, after paying the expense of keeping up their circulating capital, may not afford them average profits on their whole capital. They will, in fact, continue to work them as long as they receive, or hope to receive, average profits on their circulating capital, even though their fixed capital should return them no profit whatever.

The general result of all these observations is, that the durability of silver, and, consequently, the small proportion which the annual supply and waste bear to the whole quantity in use,— the readiness with which the demand for plate and money counteract one another, the time which must elapse before new mines can be made productive, and the reluctance with which old ones are abandoned, must occasion any cause tending to increase or diminish the motives, or the labour necessary to obtain a given quantity of silver, to be of very gradual operation. Though an increase or diminution in the Mexican demand for European and Asiatic commodities, or an increase or diminution in the fertility of the Mexican mines, would increase or diminish the

motives or the labour necessary to produce a
given quantity of silver, and ultimately increase
or diminish the annual supply; yet a long period,
as we have seen, must elapse, before the diminution or increase of the quantity of money and
plate in Europe and Asia would be perceptible.
And though an increase or diminution in the
European and Asiatic demand for plate or money
would ultimately increase or diminish the annual
supply from Mexico; yet, for a considerable time,
the increased demand for the one might be supplied at the expense of the other, without producing any perceptible effect, and after the effect
became perceptible in Mexico, a further period
must elapse before it could bring new mines into
work, or cause the abandonment of old ones.

I have hitherto confined my attention to *silver*,
and I have done so, because the degree in which
it exceeds gold in quantity occasions it to be far
more generally used, both as a medium of exchange and a standard of value. It is obvious
that the same reasoning is applicable to gold.
Its value, like that of silver, must depend on the
whole amount which is demanded, and on the

sacrifices which are required to enable that amount to be supplied. If the taste for gold trinkets were to increase ; if, for instance, solid gold buttons were indispensable parts of every gentleman's dress, or if it were possible that the long-sought *aurum potabile* could be discovered, and it should prove to be the universal medicine which the chemists of the middle ages expected, it is probable that the whole existing annual supply of gold would not be equal to the annual waste in jewellery, buttons, and medicine. The immediate consequence of the new demand would be, that a considerable part of the gold now used for money would be applied to other purposes. The value of gold would rise, and the gold still in use as money, though less in quantity, would bear the same value as the whole amount of gold money bore before. More labour would be applied to the production of gold, and, as soon as the quantity annually produced equalled the quantity annually consumed, the value of gold would again become stationary, but at a higher point, with respect to silver and all other commodities, than it stands at now.

If, on the other hand, the demand for gold trinkets and plate were to diminish, if the whole Christian world were to adopt a quakerlike simplicity of dress and furniture, a great deal of gold would be withdrawn from ornamental employment, and would be used as money. The value of gold would fall, and the whole amount of gold employed as money, though more in quantity, would bear the same value as the smaller quantity, bore before. Less labour would be employed in the production of gold, or rather its production would be suspended, until the annual waste, uncompensated by any annual supply, should have so reduced its quantity, and increased its value, as to allow its production to be recommenced. The production and consumption would then again balance one another, and the value of gold would again be stationary, though at a lower point, both with respect to silver and to all other commodities, than it stands at now.

Similar results would of course follow, if, without any previous increase or diminution of demand, there should be a diminution or increase of the annual supply. It must be remembered, however, that in consequence of the greater care that is taken of gold than of silver, and of its being less susceptible of loss from attrition or decomposition, the existing stock bears a greater proportion to the periodical production. Its value, therefore, is less affected by irregularities of supply. On the other hand, it is more affected by irregularities of demand. In times of civil commotion it is more hoarded by individuals: in war it is more wanted by governments. Its value, therefore, during long periods is more stationary, and, during short periods, less stationary than that of silver.

It has been supposed that an alteration in the supply, either of gold or silver, would affect the general value, not only of the metal in which the alteration took place, but also of the other metal. If they were mutually substitutes for each other, like the silver of Europe and America, unquestionably it would be so. But with the exception of watch-cases and lace, gold and silver, when used as commodities, are scarcely ever applied to the same purposes. We see few trinkets or picture-frames of silver, or spoons or forks of gold. Nor

is it likely that there will ever be such an alteration in the respective supplies of the two metals,
as to ornament our side-boards with gold, or our
walls with silver. And until this takes place, the
abundance of gold, though it would cheapen
trinkets and gilding, would not supply the place,
or diminish the want of silver plate; and the
abundance of silver, though it might banish pewter,
would leave the demand for gold chains and
gilding unaffected. And we have seen that the
value of a metal, as money, depends on its value
as a commodity. If we suppose a nation using a
currency composed of both metals, for instance,
of 1,000 ounces of gold and 15,000 ounces of
silver, the value of gold being 15 times that of
silver, and an increased supply of gold to reduce
its value to only ten times that of silver, 1,500
ounces of gold would be only of the same value
as the 1,000 ounces were before; prices in gold
would rise 50 per cent.; prices in silver would
remain unaltered; and neither more nor less silver
money would be required than before. And it
is scarcely necessary to state, that if we suppose
a nation to use only one of the metals as money,

its prices would be affected solely by an alteration in the value of that one metal.

The only case in which I can imagine an alteration in the general value of one metal to affect the general value of the other, is in a country using both metals equally as money, and prescribing an unvarying proportion for their mutual exchange. Suppose the currency of that country to consist, as before, of 1,000 ounces of gold and 15,000 ounces of silver, and suppose it to be penal to exchange the metals in any different proportion than one to fifteen, or to refuse payment in either metal. In such a country, if an additional supply of gold should sink the value of gold over the whole world to only ten times that of silver, all payments would, as far as possible, be made in gold; silver would become useless as coin, except for those small payments to which gold is inapplicable; the bulk of the silver coin would be melted down and exported to those countries in which it was allowed to exchange for gold in a fair proportion, and it would be difficult even to retain sufficient for fractional payments; more gold would become necessary, and, to a slight degree, the value of gold would be raised rather higher, and that of silver sink rather lower, over the whole world, than their natural proportions. Such was, to a certain extent, the policy of this country until the present century. Both metals were a legal tender, and their proportions were by law invariable; whenever, therefore, the natural proportion varied from the legal one, one of the metals went out of circulation. We have now made gold the only legal tender for all sums above 40 shillings, and though we have not, perhaps, assimilated the proportion in which gold and silver money exchange to the general proportion in the European world, we find no difficulty in keeping a currency composed of both metals.

The last general remark which occurs to me on the respective values of gold and silver is, that as gold is principally obtained by unskilled labour unassisted by capital, and silver requires for its production more skill and abstinence than almost any other commodity, the value of silver, as compared with gold, may be expected constantly to sink in the progress of improvement.

And such has actually been the case. In Europe, gold is to silver as about 1 to 15; in Asia, about 1 to 10; in Japan it is said to be about 1 to 8; at the commencement of the christian era it is supposed to have been about 1 to 10; two centuries ago it was about 1 to 14; and it is not improbable that, at the beginning of the next century, it may be 1 to 20.

I have now concluded the discussion of the causes which decide what shall be the cost of production of the precious metals in the places where they are originally obtained. But a more interesting, and a less intricate question still remains : namely, the causes which decide at what expense they shall be imported into those countries in which they are not originally obtained.*

* The Three Lectures completing this course are printed, being those on the Cost of obtaining Money.

THE END.